WHAT A WORRIED HUMAN NEEDS TO KNOW:ARTIFICIAL INTELLIGENCE

Second Edition

Andrew Corley

CONTENTS

PREFACE

Welcome to a journey that will demystify the world of AI and empower you to harness its transformative potential. Artificial intelligence has emerged as a game-changer across various industries and sectors in today's rapidly evolving technological landscape. However, it's common for non-technical individuals to feel overwhelmed or uncertain about navigating this complex field.

This book is designed with you in mind – the curious and ambitious non-technical professional eager to understand AI and explore its applications. Together, we will embark on a quest to uncover the fundamental concepts, practical insights, and ethical considerations surrounding AI. By the end of this book, you will gain the knowledge and confidence to embrace AI and leverage its capabilities to drive innovation and success in your domain.

Throughout our exploration, we will delve into the most critical questions surrounding AI. We will address key topics and provide clear, concise answers to help you develop a comprehensive understanding of this transformative technology. Some of the critical questions we will explore include:

What exactly is AI, and how does it differ from traditional computing?

What are the different types of AI, and how do they impact our daily lives?

How does machine learning work, and what are its applications in various industries?

What ethical considerations arise from AI development and deployment, and how can we navigate them responsibly?

How does bias manifest in AI systems, and what are the consequences? How can we mitigate and address bias?

What is the impact of AI on employment, and what opportunities and challenges does it present in the workplace?

How can AI revolutionize healthcare, and what are the potential implications for patient care and medical advancements?

What role does AI play in shaping Society, and how can we ensure its positive impact while addressing potential risks?

By exploring these questions and more, we will empower you to become an informed advocate and strategic thinker in AI. This book is your guide to demystifying the complexities, understanding the possibilities, and navigating the ethical considerations of AI.

So, join me on this exciting journey as we unravel the mysteries of AI and unlock its full potential. Together, let's explore the transformative power of artificial intelligence and shape a future where AI enhances the human experience in profound and meaningful ways.

CHAPTER 1:
INTRODUCTION TO AI

As we proceed through this book, we'll find that AI is a powerful tool. Amazing, frightening, and very powerful. The thing to keep in mind is Don't Panic! It can be overwhelming to understand what AI can, cannot, and should not do, which is why I decided to write this book. My goal is to explain in non-technical terms what we know about AI. I do delve into some of the mechanics of AI, but only in general, non-technical terms. Suppose you're looking for a deeper, technical understanding of this topic. In that case, many good books are available to you on Amazon.

What is Artificial Intelligence?

Artificial intelligence (AI) is a branch of computer science that creates intelligent agents. These systems can reason, learn, and act autonomously. AI research has successfully developed effective techniques for solving various problems, from game playing to medical diagnosis.

How has AI developed over time?

The field of AI research can be traced back to the early 1950s when a group of scientists at Dartmouth College held a conference on "artificial intelligence." This conference aimed to explore creating machines that could think like humans.

Early AI research focused on developing symbolic AI systems that represent and reason about the world using symbols and rules. However, these systems needed to be improved in their ability to perform complex tasks and make decisions based on uncertain information.

In the 1980s, there was a resurgence of interest in AI research, driven by the development of new machine learning algorithms. Machine learning algorithms allow computers to learn from data without being explicitly programmed. This led to the developing of more powerful AI systems that could perform tasks such as image recognition and natural language processing.

In recent years, there has been rapid growth in AI, driven by the availability of large amounts of data and the development of powerful computing systems. AI is now used in various applications, from self-driving cars to medical diagnosis.

What is the Current State of AI Technology?

The current state of AI technology is rapidly evolving. AI systems are becoming more powerful and capable of performing a more comprehensive range of tasks. Some of the most promising areas of AI research include:

Natural language processing: AI systems that can understand and generate human language.

Computer vision: AI systems that can see and understand the world around them.

Robotics: AI systems that can move and interact with the physical world.

Machine learning: AI systems that can learn from data without being explicitly programmed.

What are the Potential Benefits of AI?

AI has the potential to benefit Society in many ways. For example, AI can be used to:

Improve healthcare: AI can diagnose diseases, develop new treatments, and personalize patient care.

Improve education: AI can create personalized learning experiences, provide student feedback, and automate grading.

Improve transportation: AI can be used to develop self-driving cars, improve traffic flow, and reduce accidents.

Improve energy efficiency: AI can optimize energy use in homes and businesses, create new renewable energy sources, and reduce pollution.

What are the Ethical Concerns about AI?

While AI has the potential to benefit Society, there are also ethical concerns that need to be considered. Some of the most pressing ethical problems about AI include:

Bias: AI systems can be biased if trained on biased data. This can lead to discrimination against certain groups of people.

Job displacement: AI systems can automate tasks currently performed by humans. This could lead to job displacement and unemployment.

Privacy: AI systems can collect and store large amounts of data about people. This raises concerns about privacy and security.

AI is a rapidly evolving field with the potential to benefit Society in many ways. However, there are also ethical concerns that need to be considered. It is crucial to have a thoughtful discussion about AI's potential benefits and risks before this technology is widely adopted.

CHAPTER 2:
TYPES OF AI

Y ou might already have been using narrow AI for quite some time. Examples of narrow AI include Apple's Siri and Amazon's Alexa. These systems are very good at completing the set of tasks they're programmed to finish but, for now, won't give you the rich content that general AI could provide.

What are the Types of AI?

Artificial intelligence (AI) can be classified into different types based on capabilities, learning abilities, and goals: Narrow AI; General AI; Symbolic AI; and Subsymbolic AI. Understanding the different types of AI is essential to grasp the current capabilities of AI and where it is headed in the Future.

What is Narrow AI?

Narrow AI, also known as weak AI, refers to AI systems designed to perform a specific task, such as voice or image recognition. Narrow AI systems are programmed to perform a particular task with high accuracy. Still, they can only accomplish this task within their specific domain. For example, a narrow AI system designed to recognize faces will not be able to understand or respond to natural language.

answer it.

Here are some additional examples of NLP in practice:

Chatbots: Chatbots are computer programs that can simulate conversations with humans. They are often used in customer service applications to answer questions and provide support.

Virtual assistants: Virtual assistants are like chatbots but are designed to be more personal and helpful. They can set alarms, make appointments, and control smart home devices.

Content moderation: NLP moderates content on social media and other websites. This helps to identify and remove harmful or inappropriate content.

Fraud detection: NLP is used to detect fraudulent activity, such as credit card fraud and insurance fraud. This helps to protect businesses and individuals from financial loss.

NLP, a remarkable technology, holds immense potential to revolutionize our interactions with computers for the better. With continuous advancements in NLP algorithms, we can anticipate increasingly profound transformations in our daily lives. Harnessing the power of NLP, we are poised to witness significant enhancements in how we communicate, access information, and accomplish tasks. Let us embrace NLP's possibilities and anticipate a future where our interactions with computers are seamless, intuitive, and empowering.

CHAPTER 6:
COMPUTER VISION

S elf-driving cars use computer vision. Eight cameras are mounted on the car for Tesla vehicles compatible with self-driving features. These cameras present a surround-view of the environment. The car's onboard processing system detects and responds to environmental changes using computer vision.

What is Computer Vision?

Computer vision is a field of computer science that deals with extracting meaningful information from digital images or videos. It is a subfield of artificial intelligence that enables computers to "see" and understand the world around them.

What are the Challenges of Computer Vision?

Computer vision is a challenging field due to the complexity of natural images. Natural images are often cluttered and noisy and can be hard to interpret. Additionally, computer vision algorithms must be able to handle a wide variety of object appearances, lighting conditions, and camera angles.

Another challenge of computer vision is the need for extensive training data. Computer vision algorithms are typically trained on large datasets of labeled images. However, collecting and labeling this data can take time and effort.

How is Computer Vision Used in Practice?

Despite the challenges, computer vision has many practical applications. Here are some examples of computer vision in practice:

Self-driving cars: Computer vision is used in self-driving cars to help them navigate their surroundings and avoid obstacles. Self-driving vehicles use cameras to capture images of the road and the surrounding environment. These images are then processed by computer vision algorithms to identify objects such as cars, pedestrians, and traffic lights. The algorithms also use the images to estimate the distance to things and to track the movement of objects. This information is then used to control the car's speed and direction.

Medical imaging: Computer vision is used to help doctors diagnose diseases and injuries. Computer vision algorithms analyze medical images such as X-rays, MRI, and CT scans. These algorithms can identify abnormalities in medical images, such as tumors, and provide doctors with information about the location and size of these abnormalities.

Quality control: Computer vision is used to inspect products for defects. Computer vision algorithms are used to analyze images of products to identify defects such as cracks, scratches, and missing parts. This information can then be used to improve the quality of products.

Security: Computer vision is used in security to monitor suspicious activity. Computer vision algorithms analyze images from security cameras to identify potential threats, such as people loitering in areas where they should not be or people carrying weapons. This information can then be used to alert security guards or to take other actions to prevent a crime from happening.

Entertainment: Computer vision creates special effects and augmented reality experiences. Computer vision algorithms track the movement of objects and people in real-time. This information can then be used to create special effects, such as objects that float in mid-air or people who seem to be interacting with virtual objects. Computer vision is also used to create augmented reality experiences, which allow users to interact with virtual objects in the real world.

Computer vision, a remarkable technology, holds immense potential to positively and transform various aspects of our lives. As computer vision algorithms advance, we can expect significant healthcare, transportation, security, and entertainment enhancements. From improving medical diagnoses to enabling autonomous vehicles, computer vision opens doors to new possibilities and experiences. Let us embrace the exciting journey ahead, where the power of computer vision enhances our understanding of the world, simplifies tasks, and enriches our daily lives.

CHAPTER 7:
ETHICS AND AI

D eep fakes are a real thing. Deep fakes use AI-generated voice-overs that are very accurate to the original voice. These can be used for comedic purposes, and I've seen several that are very funny (funny being a relative term). However, these can be used for fraud, such as "your CFO" calling to confirm the $250,000 wire transfer they emailed you about. However, the email and the voice were both faked.

Artificial intelligence (AI) is a rapidly developing technology with the potential to revolutionize many aspects of our lives. However, as AI becomes more powerful, it is essential to consider the ethical implications of its development and use.

What are the Ethical Dilemmas in AI?

Many ethical dilemmas can arise in the development and use of AI. Some of the most common ethical dilemmas include:

Bias: AI systems are only as good as the data they are trained on. If the data is biased, the AI system will also be biased. This can lead to discrimination against certain groups of people.

Automation: AI systems can automate many tasks that are currently done by humans. This could lead to widespread job loss and economic inequality.

Decision-making: AI systems can decide who gets a loan or is hired for a job. If these decisions are not made fairly and transparently, it could lead to injustice.

Privacy: AI systems can collect and analyze large amounts of data about people. This data could track people's movements, monitor online activity, or predict future behavior. This raises concerns about privacy and surveillance.

Security: AI systems can be hacked or manipulated. This could lead to the misuse of AI for malicious purposes, such as spreading misinformation or propaganda or even carrying out cyberattacks.

Are There Potential Solutions to These Ethical Challenges?

There are many potential solutions to the ethical challenges of AI. Some of the most promising solutions include:

Transparency: AI systems should be transparent so people can understand how they work and make decisions. This can help to ensure that AI systems are not used in a discriminatory or unfair way.

Fairness: AI systems should be designed to be fair and unbiased. This means that they should not discriminate against any particular group of people.

Accountability: AI systems should be accountable for their decisions. This means there should be a way to hold the developers and users of AI systems responsible for the consequences of their actions.

Regulation: Governments and other regulatory bodies can develop rules that govern the development and use of AI. These regulations can ensure that AI is used safely and ethically.

Education: The public needs to be educated about the ethical challenges of AI. This will help people to understand the potential risks and benefits of AI and to make informed decisions about its use.

Can Safeguards be built directly into AI systems?

Asimov's Laws of Robotics are a set of safeguard principles first introduced by science fiction writer Isaac Asimov in his works. While these laws were initially created for storytelling purposes, they have sparked discussions and influenced the development of ethical guidelines for AI systems.

When applying these principles to AI, it's important to note that they serve as a conceptual framework rather than direct guidelines for AI development. They reflect the ethical considerations and responsibilities of designing AI systems to interact with humans.

The First Law: *A robot may not injure a human being or, through inaction, allow a human being to come to harm.* In the context of AI, this principle emphasizes the importance of ensuring the safety and well-being of humans. AI systems should be designed with safeguards to minimize the risk of harm to individuals, both physically and mentally.

The Second Law: *A robot must obey the orders given to it by human beings except where such orders would conflict with the First Law.* This principle highlights the need for AI systems to respect human authority and follow instructions as long as those instructions do not contradict the First Law. It underscores the importance of human oversight and control over AI technology.

The Third Law: *A robot must protect its own existence as long as such protection does not conflict with the First or Second Law.* This principle recognizes the need for self-preservation in AI systems as long as it does not compromise the safety and well-being of humans or violate human commands. It implies that AI systems should be designed to prevent harm to themselves, but not at the expense of human welfare.

Asimov's later addition of the Fourth Law, also known as the Zeroth Law, expanded the scope of ethical considerations in AI:

The Zeroth Law: *A robot may not harm **humanity** or, by inaction, allow humanity to come to harm.* This law prioritizes the broader welfare of humanity over individual humans. It implies that AI systems should contribute to humanity's greater good, considering long-term consequences and societal impacts.

Applying these principles to AI development requires careful consideration of ethical implications, transparency, accountability, and ensuring that AI systems align with human values. Ethical guidelines and frameworks, such as those developed by organizations like the IEEE and OpenAI, aim to address these concerns and promote responsible AI development.

It is important to remember that AI is a powerful technology that can be used for good or bad. It is up to us to ensure that AI is developed and used ethically. By implementing these solutions, we can ensure that AI is developed and used ethically.

CHAPTER 8: BIAS IN AI

E xamples of bias in AI are not hard to find. One example is the case of a large technology company's recruitment algorithm, which was developed to sift through resumés and identify top candidates for jobs. The algorithm was trained on resumés submitted to the company over 10 years, mostly from men. As a result, the algorithm learned to favor male candidates over female candidates. The company ultimately scrapped the project.

Bias in AI refers to the systematic errors or inaccuracies in the decisions made by AI algorithms, which result in unfair or discriminatory outcomes. Bias can occur at any stage of the AI development process, from data collection to algorithm design and deployment.

What Causes Bias in AI?

There are several causes of bias in AI. One of the most common causes is biased data. AI algorithms learn from the data they are trained on, and if that data is biased, the algorithm will also be biased. For example, suppose an AI algorithm is trained on data that only includes images of lighter-skinned people. In that case, it may have difficulty accurately recognizing darker-skinned individuals.

Another cause of bias is the lack of diversity in the teams that develop AI systems. If the team developing an AI system is homogeneous, they may need to be aware of biases affecting specific groups. This can result in AI systems that work well for some people rather than for others.

Are there Consequences of AI Bias?

The consequences of bias in AI can be severe, particularly for marginalized groups. For example, suppose a facial recognition algorithm is biased against people with darker skin tones. In that case, it may result in innocent individuals being wrongfully accused of crimes. Similarly, if an AI algorithm used for job recruitment is biased against women, it could result in qualified women being passed over for jobs.

Have there been Examples of AI Bias?

An example of bias in AI is the use of facial recognition technology by law enforcement agencies. Studies have shown that these algorithms are more likely to misidentify people with darker skin tones, leading to false arrests and wrongful convictions.

Another example of bias in AI is the use of AI in lending. Studies have shown that AI algorithms to assess creditworthiness are more likely to deny loans to people of color, even with the same financial qualifications as white borrowers.

How is Bias in AI addressed?

Addressing bias in AI is essential for ensuring that AI systems are fair and do not discriminate against certain groups. One potential solution is to ensure that AI development teams are diverse and represent a range of perspectives. Additionally, AI systems should be audited regularly to identify and address biases. Also, the underlying data set should be crafted to be diverse.

Bias in AI is a serious issue that needs to be addressed. AI development teams must ensure that their systems are fair and do not discriminate against certain groups. By doing so, we can harness the power of AI to make the world a better and more equitable place.

CHAPTER 9: AI AND THE WORKPLACE

I've wanted to write a book for a while and now have the time and the resources to do so. Given the current popularity of the AI topic, I decided to pull the trigger and write a book on AI. The best part about this process is that I used AI to help build the topic list and to write content.

Artificial Intelligence (AI) is rapidly transforming the workplace. From automating repetitive tasks to making complex decisions, AI is changing how we work. This chapter will explore the impact of AI on employment, its applications in the workplace, and the potential implications for the Future of work.

What is AI's Impact on Employment?

One of the most significant impacts of AI on employment is the potential for job displacement. AI is already being used to automate many tasks that were once performed by humans, such as data entry, customer service, and manufacturing. As AI continues to develop, even more jobs will likely be automated. This could lead to significant job losses, particularly in routine and repetitive occupations.

However, AI is also creating new jobs. AI-powered technologies are being used to develop new products and services, which creates new demand for workers with specialized skills. For example, AI is being used to develop self-driving cars, creating new jobs in the automotive industry. AI is also used to develop new medical treatments, creating jobs in the healthcare industry.

Overall, the impact of AI on employment is complex and uncertain. While AI is likely to lead to job displacement in some occupations, it is also expected to create new jobs in other fields. The net impact of AI on employment will depend on several factors, including the pace of technological development, the availability of training programs, and the overall state of the economy.

How is AI used in the Workplace?

AI is already being used in a variety of ways in the workplace. For example, AI is being used to:

Automate repetitive tasks, such as data entry and customer service;

Make complex decisions, such as loan approvals and medical diagnoses;

Develop new products and services; Improve efficiency and productivity;

Personalize customer experiences; And

Analyze data and identify trends.

The applications of AI in the Workplace are constantly evolving. As AI technology develops, we can expect to see even more innovative and impactful uses of AI in the Workplace.

What are the Implications for the Future of Work?

Previous automation advances have had a mixed impact on workforce employment. Some jobs have been eliminated altogether, while others have been transformed. For example, the introduction of assembly lines led to the elimination of many manufacturing jobs. However, it also created new engineering, design, and marketing jobs.

The impact of automation on employment is typically gradual. It can take years for new technologies to be adopted and even longer for them to significantly affect the workforce. For example, the first automated teller machines (ATMs) were introduced in the 1970s. Still, it was in the 1990s that they began to have a significant impact on bank teller jobs.

The impact of AI on employment is likely to be similar. It will take time for AI to become sophisticated enough to automate many of the tasks currently done by humans. However, once it does, it is likely to significantly impact the workforce.

The good news is that AI is also likely to create new jobs. For example, AI will be needed to develop and maintain AI systems. It will also be required to train and retrain workers for new jobs. In addition, AI will create new opportunities in research, development, and marketing.

The implications of AI for the Future of work are significant. As AI becomes more prevalent in the workplace, workers must adapt to new technologies and acquire new skills to remain competitive. This will require substantial investments in workforce training and education programs. Additionally, AI will create new ethical and social challenges that must be addressed, such as the impact on human workers and the potential for bias and discrimination in AI algorithms.

Despite the challenges, AI also has the potential to create a more efficient, productive, and equitable workplace. By automating repetitive tasks, AI can free workers to focus on more creative and strategic work. AI can also improve decision-making, personalize customer experiences, and identify trends. AI can help create a brighter work future by addressing the challenges and seizing the opportunities.

CHAPTER 10: AI AND HEALTHCARE

We recently experienced a situation that caused us concern that could have been avoided. During an outpatient registration event, a family member was given an EKG. The healthcare providers became concerned about the results and reported the likelihood of a severe cardiac event. It took us two weeks to get an appointment with our primary care provider, who explained there was no cause for concern. She walked us through the EKG read-out and explained why it wasn't a concern. The EKG read-out automated text indicated a likely cardiac event. Still, an AI could have evaluated the readings more closely to the skill of a trained physician (and saved us a false call-out and two weeks of worry).

Artificial intelligence (AI) has the potential to revolutionize healthcare by transforming the way healthcare professionals diagnose, treat, and prevent diseases. AI can help healthcare providers make faster, more accurate, and more personalized decisions. Here, we will discuss the potential applications of AI in healthcare, provide examples of AI in healthcare in practice, and outline potential implications for the Future of healthcare.

What are the Potential Applications of AI in Healthcare?

AI has numerous potential applications in healthcare. One

primary application is in medical imaging, where AI algorithms can analyze medical images, such as CT scans, MRIs, and X-rays, and help identify abnormalities that might be difficult for a human to detect. AI can also help healthcare professionals identify early signs of diseases by analyzing patterns in data from medical records, lab reports, and genetic tests.

Another application of AI in healthcare is drug discovery. AI can analyze vast amounts of data on genetic variations, chemical compounds, and drug interactions to identify potential new drugs or repurpose existing ones for new uses. AI algorithms can also help healthcare professionals optimize patient treatment plans by predicting how patients will respond to treatments based on their medical histories and genetic profiles.

AI can also be used to develop and improve medical devices. For example, AI algorithms can analyze data from wearable devices, such as fitness trackers and smartwatches, to identify patterns and detect abnormalities that could indicate potential health issues. AI can also help improve surgical procedures by enabling surgeons to visualize anatomy in real-time, allowing them to perform operations with greater accuracy and precision.

Are there Examples of AI in Healthcare in Practice?

AI is already being used in numerous healthcare applications. For instance, researchers at Stanford University developed an AI algorithm that can detect skin cancer as accurately as dermatologists. The algorithm was trained on more than 130,000 images of skin lesions. It identified skin cancer with an accuracy rate of 91%.

Another example of AI in healthcare is IBM's Watson for Oncology. This AI-powered tool helps healthcare professionals develop personalized cancer treatment plans. Watson for Oncology uses natural language processing to analyze medical records, clinical guidelines, and other relevant data to recommend treatment options tailored to each patient's unique needs.

AI also improves patient outcomes in intensive care units (ICUs). Researchers at Johns Hopkins University developed an AI system that analyzes real-time data from patient monitors and electronic medical records to predict when a patient is at risk of sepsis, a life-threatening complication of infection. The system has helped reduce the number of deaths from the condition by alerting healthcare providers when patients are at risk of sepsis.

What are the Potential Implications for the Future of Healthcare?

The use of AI in healthcare has the potential to significantly improve patient outcomes by enabling faster, more accurate diagnoses and more personalized treatment plans. However, there are also potential ethical and social implications to consider.

One concern is that AI could widen existing healthcare disparities. AI algorithms may not be trained on diverse populations, which could result in biased or inaccurate diagnoses and treatments for certain groups of people. Additionally, AI may be more accessible to those with the means to pay for it, further exacerbating existing inequalities in healthcare.

Another concern is that using AI in healthcare may lead to dehumanization, with patients feeling like they are being treated by machines rather than human healthcare providers. This could have implications for patient trust and satisfaction with healthcare.

Despite these concerns, the potential benefits of AI in healthcare are significant, and the technology is likely to play an increasingly important role in the Future of healthcare. As AI continues to develop, it is crucial to know its potential ethical and social implications and take steps to mitigate these risks.

CHAPTER 11: AI AND SOCIETY

Artificial intelligence (AI) is a rapidly developing technology that has the potential to revolutionize many aspects of our lives. AI is already used in various ways, from healthcare to finance to transportation. As AI continues to develop, it will likely have an even more significant impact on Society.

At breakfast one morning, my wife asked whether AI could be used for illegal purposes. I told her yes, definitely. Any tool that gets work done faster and more accurately can be used for good and BAD outcomes. We'll see more of that as AI takes a greater hold on our Society.

What are the potential impacts of AI on Society?

One of AI's most significant impacts is likely on the job market. As AI becomes more sophisticated, it can automate many tasks humans currently do. This could lead to widespread job loss, particularly in industries heavily reliant on manual labor. However, AI will also likely create new jobs, as it will be needed to develop and maintain AI systems.

Another significant impact of AI is how we live our lives. AI-powered devices and services could make our lives more convenient and efficient. For example, AI-powered home assistants could help us set alarms, turn on lights, and order groceries. AI could also be used to improve our health and well-being. For example, AI-powered medical devices could help us to diagnose and treat diseases more effectively.

AI is also likely to have a significant impact on the way we interact with each other. AI-powered chatbots could be used to provide customer service, education, and entertainment. AI could also create new forms of social media and communication platforms.

Overall, AI has the potential to bring about significant benefits to Society. However, being aware of AI's potential risks and challenges is vital. These risks include the potential for AI to be used for malicious purposes, the potential for AI to create economic inequality, and the potential for AI to harm our privacy and security. It is essential to work to address these risks and challenges to ensure that AI is developed and used responsibly and ethically.

How is AI affecting Society today?

Here are some specific examples of how AI is being used in Society today:

In **healthcare**, AI is used to develop new drugs and treatments, diagnose diseases, and provide personalized care. For example, AI analyzes medical images to identify cancer cells and develop customized treatment plans for cancer patients.

In **finance**, AI analyzes market data, makes investment decisions, and manages risk in finance. For example, AI predicts stock prices and develops trading algorithms that automatically buy and sell stocks.

In **transportation**, AI improves traffic flow, develops autonomous vehicles, and enhances safety. For example, AI is being used to create algorithms that can automatically control traffic lights and to develop autonomous vehicles that can safely navigate roads.

In **customer service**, AI is being used to provide personalized support, answer questions, and resolve issues. For example, AI is used to develop chatbots that can answer customer questions and create algorithms that automatically resolve customer issues.

In **education**, AI personalizes learning, provides feedback, and grades assignments. For example, AI is used to develop personalized learning plans for students and algorithms that can automatically grade essays and other assignments.

In **entertainment**, AI creates new forms of content, personalizes recommendations, and generates interactive experiences. For example, AI is being used to develop new video game forms and algorithms that can automatically generate personalized recommendations for movies and TV shows.

These are just a few examples of how AI is used in Society today. As AI continues to develop, it will likely have an even more significant impact on our lives. It is essential to be aware of the potential benefits and risks of AI so that we can work to ensure that it is developed and used responsibly and ethically.

CHAPTER 12: THE FUTURE OF AI

As technology advances, so does the development of artificial intelligence (AI). The Future of AI is constantly evolving and presents both challenges and opportunities. This chapter will discuss the current and future trends in AI development, provide an overview of where AI is heading, and discuss potential challenges and opportunities in the Future of AI. We'll see more trends in AI, good and bad, as we gain more experience using it. If you hear the term "emergent properties" used concerning AI, understand that it is the scientific way of saying, "We didn't know it could do that." With the implicit "and we need to figure out HOW it did that" left unspoken.

What are any Current Trends in AI Development?

One of the current trends in AI development is the use of deep learning algorithms to create better AI models. Deep learning models use neural networks to process and learn from large amounts of data. This has led to significant advancements in computer vision, natural language processing, and speech recognition.

Another trend is the development of AI-powered virtual assistants, chatbots, and other conversational AI tools. These tools are becoming increasingly common in customer service, healthcare, and finance industries. They can help reduce workload and improve efficiency by automating tasks and providing personalized experiences for users.

Finally, AI is used in various industries, such as finance, transportation, manufacturing, and agriculture, to improve efficiency and productivity. For example, AI-powered robots are being used in factories to perform repetitive tasks. Also, predictive analytics is being used in agriculture to optimize crop yield.

What are possible Future Trends in AI Development?

The Future of AI is heading toward developing more autonomous AI systems. These systems can learn and adapt without human intervention, making them more efficient and effective. For example, the development of autonomous vehicles is a significant trend in the Future of AI. Other areas expected to see considerable advancements include healthcare, finance, and cybersecurity.

Another trend is the development of explainable AI. Many AI systems operate as black boxes, making understanding how they arrive at their conclusions difficult. Explainable AI will enable humans to better understand the decision-making process of AI systems, making it easier to identify and correct biases and errors.

Finally, integrating AI with other emerging technologies, such as the Internet of Things (IoT) and blockchain, is expected to become more prevalent. This will enable the development of more efficient and secure data processing, storage, and analysis systems.

Are there Potential Challenges and Opportunities for AI in the Future?

As AI continues to advance, it presents challenges and opportunities for Society. One significant challenge is the potential displacement of jobs as AI becomes more integrated into industries such as manufacturing and transportation. This could lead to substantial job losses, particularly for those in low-skill and repetitive roles.

Another challenge is the potential for AI to be used negatively, such as through cyberattacks or deep fake technology. Developing regulations and ethical standards is essential to ensure that AI is used ethically and responsibly.

On the other hand, AI presents significant opportunities for Society. For example, it can be used to improve healthcare outcomes by developing better diagnostic tools and treatments. It can also tackle global challenges such as climate change, poverty, and disease.

The Future of AI is constantly evolving, and the potential applications of AI are endless. While AI presents challenges and opportunities, it is essential to approach its development and use responsibly and ethically. By doing so, we can unlock AI's full potential and improve people's lives worldwide.

Here are some additional thoughts on the Future of AI:

AI is likely to have a profound impact on the way we live and work. It is already being used in various ways, and its capabilities will improve.

It is essential to be aware of AI's potential challenges and opportunities. We must develop regulations and ethical standards to ensure that AI is used responsibly.

AI has the potential to improve our lives in many ways. It can be used to solve some of the world's most pressing problems, such as climate change and poverty.

We need to embrace AI and use it to our advantage. It is a powerful technology that has the potential to make the world a better place.

Artificial intelligence (AI) is a rapidly developing technology with the potential to revolutionize many aspects of our lives. AI is already used in various ways, from powering self-driving cars to developing new medical treatments. As AI continues to advance, it is crucial to consider the ethical implications of its development and use.

EPILOGUE

I aimed to make this book easy to read and understand by breaking down complex topics into simple chapters. I want to clarify some of the confusion around AI and emphasize its positive impact on our lives. For e-book readers, thank you for clicking the links. That incorporates my Amazon Affiliates' information (a small commission for me on any sales you complete via that link). Please check out my Udemy Instructor Profile for information on a course on this topic and new topics coming soon!

While some people fear that AI will lead to disastrous consequences, we should approach it with cautious optimism. AI has the potential to solve many of the world's problems and make our lives easier and more efficient.

In the Future, we can expect even more advances in AI technology, including chat-based AI, that can help us daily. So watch for my next book, focusing on how you can best utilize chat-based AI.

Overall, AI is a rapidly evolving field with limitless possibilities. As we continue to develop and refine this technology, we can look forward to a brighter and more innovative future.